e.
s.
p.

poems
Michael Leong

Michael Leong pursues what he calls a "ludic inarticulacy" throughout the pages of e.s.p., and like all great adventures, the chase is as good as the capture. He's got a wonderful sense of humor, combined with a magician's ease and the biggest wand in three counties. Puns, acronyms, anagrams, plays on words abound, though in the service of some deeper feeling. It's all in what you don't see, but when the shell game's over, you'll be feeling Leong's words stitched on the inside of your pockets.

-Kevin Killian

Michael Leong is a flâneur of language, an architect of intellectual oases, a slap to the gland of boredom and easy poetry, a magician that articulates undomesticated verses with elegance and intelligence. Leong agitates the page and plays with it, he anticipates language, he folds it, he breaks it into pieces of infinite and impeccable meanings as a wise child making figures of origami.

-Estela Lamat

e.s.p.

Michael Leong

Silenced Press

e.s.p. Copyright © 2009 by Silenced Press. All rights reserved. Printed in the United States of America- Columbus, Ohio. No part of this book may be used or reproduced in any manner whatsoever without written permission except in the case of brief quotations embodied in critical articles and reviews.

First Edition.

ISBN-13: 978-0-9792410-2-4
ISBN-10: 0-9792410-2-2

Library of Congress Control Number: †

More information available at:

www.silencedpress.com

ACKNOWLEDGEMENTS

Thanks to the editors of the following journals who published versions of these poems: *Cranky Literary Journal, ditch, jubilat, La Fovea, Marginalia, NFG Magazine, Opium Magazine, Pindeldyboz, Rhapsoidia, Saint Elizabeth Street, Snow Monkey,* and *Yzur.*

TABLE OF CONTENTS

["*Suppose I wrote it in chalk*"]	1
The line lengthens	3
Poem	5
The Signals	11
OBJECTIVE	13
Pensando en la inmortalidad del cangrejo	14
Hastily Sketched Blueprint for the Last and Final Nidification	16
In lieu of a poem	20
Variations on a Pangram	22
magnetic poetry	24
Catcalls from an imaginary city	26
Acrostic for Borges' Library, or Proposal as Rube Goldberg Machine	28
"i" before "e"	29
For Estela Lamat	31
for the writers house / where the roof is rust	33
and I just stood there…	35
The Signals (2)	37
nocturne	41
Не вешай лапшу на уши	42
E.S.P.	44
It goes without saying	45
Boy Leading Horse	46
Disco Dante	47
Textbook Execution	49
Having a Hard Time of It	50
The Connoisseur	51

Untitled ("We will slam them with our wings")	52
The Signals (3)	53
I swim a sea that has no shore or bottom,	56
Se te escaparon los enanitos pa'l bosque	58
[lower east side]	67
Aviary	68
Yoshitomo Nara's Girls	69
Found Sound Poem (or Ways in Which We Communicated When, in a Former Life, We Lived Together in Ancient Egypt as Cats and Were Thus Revered as Gods)	70
Ballistic Signature	71
Still Life with Stillbirth	72
Creation Story	73
Notes Toward ~~An Elusive Allusive A Lucid~~ A Ludic Inarticulacy	74
The Signals (3.1415926535 8979323846 2643383279 5028841971 6939937510 5820974944 5923078164 0628620899 8628034825 3421 ...)	77
Aşağı tükürsem sakal, yukarı tükürsem bıyık	78
and so I imagined going...	79
until my mouth becomes my tongue's sarcophagus	83
NOTES	85

Suppose I wrote it in chalk

Suppose I wrote it in crayon, in highlighter, in colored pencil

Suppose I took a chisel and meticulously carved it in stone

Suppose I pulverized the stone into powder and carefully formed letters out of the dust

Suppose I rolled it into a cylinder and sent it shuttling through a complex network of tubes

Suppose I shut the door and turned on the shower and traced the words on the mirror with the tip of my finger

Suppose I sent it telepathically

Suppose I could convey it in its totality by a simple raising and lowering of an eyebrow

Suppose I turned on the shower again

              and let the words emerge on their own

Suppose I gave you an ear trumpet and you gave me a megaphone

Suppose I had telekinesis and could drag the point of

1

*that pencil over that sheet of paper to make a series
of marks which you could then interpret as signs*

*Suppose we were separated by a wall on which we could
  tap out messages in Morse code*

*Suppose we copiloted a plane with which we could
  skywrite it in secret at night*

Suppose I constructed crop circles,

    gigantic glyphs the size

        of the Nazca Lines

Suppose I told a certain person

    who could disseminate it through the grapevine

Suppose I exhaled smoke signals—
        for your inhalation only

*Suppose I climbed to the top of a mountain and screamed
  it at the top of my lungs;*

    suppose that the echo   could last

        and carry it

            carry it   for miles

The line lengthens

but leads nowhere—it broods in an abyss of its own abeyance—it twists against the tug of its teleology—it luxuriates in the cul-de-sacs of its very lassitude (thereby belying the logic of its own linearity)—nevertheless, it lurches forward through labored, illogical linkages, wishing that, in fact, it were part of a grid, pining for points of contact, to be pierced, to be bisected by numerous lines while longing for a surplus of counterparts, of complementary lines that would parallel every step of its way without ever meeting—the line gets lost, derailed by its own ramifying train of thought, and reappears, as The Tropic of Cancer, as a tight-rope walker's tenuous vector, as a bridge over Heraclitus' river, as the shortest distance between eternity and never, as the impossible cord that connects the tin can cupped to my mouth to the tin can pressed against your ear, as a news ticker on some pirate channel that streams headlines like "Roller coasters were once the backbones of dinosaurs" and "L---g last seen lurking behind the crumbling crenellations of the night"—the line longs to be plucked, to be set vibrating, to be, in truth, not just a single tone but a note humming amidst a harmonious chord—but the line, in spite of itself, abhors breakage, fears enjambment and the pain of a period—in short, it longs to go on, in a state of circular self sufficiency, and so, by becoming a looping Ouroborean being, that is, by swallowing its own tail, the line—in its lonely longevity—lengthens

Poem

1.

Before reading this poem,
rise and go out into the streets!

Then go back inside, making sure
to leave the door ajar.

2.

Before reading this poem, say,
"Strange…these aren't

the parts I ordered."
Say it again in a different way.

3.

Window-shop
before reading this poem.

Study the second hand
of a second hand clock.

4.

Get an enema
before reading this poem—
but only if you want to.

5.

Before reading this poem,

smear the page
          with a layer of lard.

Then hold it up to the light.

6.

Before reading this poem,
go for a day
without saying the word "I,"
the word "you,"
the word "poem."

7.

Before reading this poem,
write one yourself.

Try to make it better than this.

8.

Hold your breath before reading this poem—
don't let it out till the end.

9.

Before reading this poem,
tie your right arm to the chair.

10.

Before reading this poem,
tie your left arm to the table

11.

Before reading this poem,
have your neighbor read it
and paraphrase it for you.

Type up a transcript and title it "Poem."

Commit it to memory,
                back it up on disk.

12.

Before reading this poem,
dust it for prints.

Handle it gingerly with pincers.

13.

Stand before a mirror before
reading this poem.

Perform sets of deep knee bends
without laughing.

14.

Try to trade it.

15.

Before reading this poem,
think of everything else you could be doing.

Type up the list and title it "Poem."

16.

Before reading this poem,
listen.

    Can you hear the words
becoming vestigial?

17.

Ante up before reading this poem.

Stagger your thoughts
accordingly.

18.

Before reading this poem,
pick an understudy.

Call in sick, take a vow
of silence.

19.

Expect the best
before reading this poem.

Feign disappointment
when it's done.

20.

Before reading this poem,
read another poem.

Read another and another.
Then tell me what you think the difference is.

21.

Before reading this poem,
preheat your oven,

but don't expect the poem to feed you.

The Signals

The signals…　　you know,
　the ones that you sent me—

　　　with what contagion　　did they fluoresce
in the fjords of my brain?

　　　　　with what sutural inscription
　　　　　with what　　curdled election
　　　　　with　　what caulk
　　　　　　　and suction
　　　　　with　　　what fulminating forms
　　　　　　　of　felined flexion　?

The signals, the ones you sent me—
　　in which crucible
　did they achieve
　　　　　their circumambient coagulation
their　irrigated　reticulation

　　　　their spasmodic swaths
of　forked　threnody　?

　　　　in which　clotted chalice
　　in which
　　　　　　fallen
　　　　　caldera

in which   vent
in which   faucet
in which   streaming

                socket

                        of   possibility   ?

OBJECTIVE

> Remember that while it's great to have an open mind regarding your objective, an unclear objective can pose a problem when developing your resume.
> —Kim Isaacs, Monster Resume Expert, monster.com

To proceed by means of in(ter)ference.
To load every rift with "or."
To realign the spine of the times and see—with my third eye—the writhing on the wall.
To write a pantoum called "Pandora's Tomb."
To play a pinball machine named "Sisyphus."
To recklessly and indiscriminately use The Unheimlich Maneuver, and when questioned, to back away and feign that I'm choking.
To catch the thick of things that always seems to slip through the cracks.
To woo the words out of the woodwork.
To take the woodwork apart and reassemble it as a Trojan horse in which the words can patiently wait within the gates of the city.

Pensando en la inmortalidad del cangrejo

["Thinking about the immortality of the crab" is a Spanish idiom that refers to daydreaming.]

I'm thinking about the immortality of the crab,
about where it goes once it has shed
its earthly carapace—
                      in a heaven far
from the constellation Cancer.

If I gaze into the abandoned amphitheater
of my navel,
              I can faintly make out
its crustaceous paradise,
                    its exoskeletal afterlife—

away from the scalding water and wooden mallets,
away from the metal crackers
      with their sharp, serrated edges,

      where there are no pointed little forks
or plastic bibs to shield from the splatter.

Within the oceanic O
of my *omphalos*,
the crab is dreaming
a fathomless dream about
the bottom of the sea,
where the kelp sways lazily,
and the coral feeds

at its leisure,
and, from time to time,
bursts of bubbles
unexpectedly rise
to the surface,
which, from here,
give only the slightest impression
that the water is boiling.

*Hastily Sketched Blueprint for the Last and
Final Nidification*

we'll go   below the radar,
   under the *whether*

     we'll find the banyans that border the bell
curve,
       the infinitesimal point
    at which
dusk
  siphons off
        into the database—

    and in the morning's shimmering
metaphorescence,

       we'll use more than one mirror
       to see the backs of our heads

    *

but but but   bursting from the branches,
    swerving
     deliriously thru the circuitry—
  alarmed birds

      perched on skyscrapers:
   descents of woodpeckers
with razor-edged bills ready to chisel—

    alarmed birds
         burgeoning in the tunnels:
   sieges of herons
on the subway
               endlessly screeching—

a congregation of birds,
a dissimulation
   of birds, an unkindness of ravens
marauding
   the airwaves—

   "Here at home, we have to continue to work
to build a unified set of effective capabilities to
manage the risk to the people"

      a scourge of birds
      with barbed-wire beaks
         "on behalf of the people"

      a deceit of lapwings
      a convocation of eagles

      a column of light
      around which
      a murder of birds is circling

                *

  but we'll hush
 and cup
      our ears
    to hear
the voices   vying in the vowelswell—
and we'll say to them: "inarticulate"
     we'll say: "a clear intuit"
         we'll say: "nautical rite"

    we'll hear
        herds of hoarseness
in the heart of hearing—
        we'll   graft
          together the gaggles of garble
gurgling
    from our gullets

and   in   *despair*
we'll find
                   e.s.p.

    we'll find

                        air

In lieu of a poem

When I sleep she scrimshaws my bones and decks my throat with garlands of dessicance. She draws dotted lines that tenuously connect The Beyond to my Organ of Corti. She suggests every six months a cosmetic lobotomy. She circles around my desk in eccentric orbits, alternating between limping and skipping. She gets into my notes, bevels every eleventh letter, and turns the left-hand margin into a Möbius strip. The creases of her dress crawl and crackle with glitches. When it rains she paints, practices calligraphy, and bides her time in the shadow box. From there, she sends me messages like:

> duh-DAH-duh-DAH-duh-DAH-duh-DAH-duh-DAH…

or:

> yr unreliable narrator
> now sleeps w/ the fishes

or:

> ☺ Your principles mean more to you
> than any money or success. ☺
> 13 22 5 28 42 46

She dreams in pig Latin. An avid renouncer, her hobbies include retraction, abjurement, disavowal, apostasy. Around her swarm half-thoughts, awkward silences, insipid tongue twisters, sentences cut short by sneezing which she seizes from the air and pins to a board like butterflies. If I protest she pretends she doesn't understand English. She laces my tea with 1/3 ambition, 2/3 lethargy. She chain smokes to mask her halitosis. She pickles my failures in jars of formaldehyde. She never takes "no" for an answer. She daintily sips from my cup clinking ice-cubes made of ink.

Variations on a Pangram

A quick brown fox jumps over the lazy dog.

A quick brown fox jumps over the lazy dog to eat the pâté.

A quick brown fox jumps over the lazy dog to eat the pâté and Mildred's Bœuf en Daube.

A quick brown fox, as fleet as *Æon Flux*, jumps over the lazy dog to eat the pâté and Mildred's Bœuf en Daube then disappears behind Þe Olde English Pub.

A quick brown fox, as fleet as *Æon Flux*, jumps over the lazy dog to eat the pâté and Mildred's Bœuf en Daube then disappears with Slavoj Žižek's llama behind Þe Olde English Pub.

A quick brown fox, as fleet as *Æon Flux*, jumps over the lazy dog to eat the pâté and Mildred's Bœuf en Daube then disappears with Slavoj Žižek's llama behind the façade of Þe Olde English Pub to sing a noël in preparation for El Niño.

As my spinning dreidel lands on ⟨w⟩, I write in my notebook—beneath quotes by Søren Kierkegaard and Czesław Miłosz, beneath a roughly drawn *Pietà* and the phrase *sunt lacrimae rērum*—the following sentence: "With considerable élan and without a soupçon of hesitation, a quick brown fox, as fleet as *Æon Flux*, jumps over the lazy dog to eat the pâté and Mildred's Bœuf en Daube then disappears with Slavoj Žižek's llama behind the façade of Þe Olde English Pub to sing a noël in preparation for El Niño."

Then below it, I pen a "ə"
to begin the poor dog's upside-down elegy.

magnetic poetry

i yearn to get   c mp
poetic name   g try
   get romantic   epy
reaction   get my   p
   panegyric tome   t
i type agon   etc mr
i try neat poem   cg
get coy print   aem
   image poetry   n tc
   myopic genre   att
   gnomic trap   eety
i trope   may get   nc
anti poetry   cgem
peyote margin   tc
   may ego trip   n etc
i tango meter   pcy
i peg my trance to
any topic   merge   t
   my ectopia   get   nr
   crypt   get anomie
entropic game   yt
me try antic ep   go
   ye optic art   m egn
gyrate open mic   t
paint geometry   c
tantric poem   eyg
tempt irony   cage
epic anger   to my   t

24

magic entry to	pe
my pent argot ie	c
my one act gripe	t
o my epic rage	tnt
tragic omen	p yet
metric agony	pte
pent atomic gyre	
o rage empty	ctn i
mantic poet	gyre
omit create	pngy

Catcalls from an imaginary city

> I'll drink your bathwater
> —Man on street to passing woman,
> New York City

I'll buy you a dress made of loose ends and infinitives
I'll ask you politely about proper conjugation
I'll break your abacus but I'll repair your sextant
I'll clean your whisper dish and always respect
   the orientation of your compass
I'll anoint your eyes with azure
I'll disinter the air you intaglio
I'll drench myself in your incipience
I'll wait in the depths of your dormancy
I'll knot the threads of your dress into miniature
   nooses
and decipher the hermetic impressions of your shoes
I'll coauthor an apocryphal version of your
   autobiography
I'll develop a penchant for the way you say "city"
I'll grovel in the magnetic grottoes of your voice
I'll trace the perfect curves of your every caesura
I'll shrink wrap your secrets
   and sentence them to death
   by hanging
I'll hold séances for your former incarnations and
   when they come I'll kiss each one of them—not just
   the pretty ones—on the crown of the head
I'll spy on you through the singing tines of a tuning
   fork

I'll list for you all the synonyms for the word
   "euphony"
and make them up if too little exist
To the best of my ability I'll help you stanch
   Time's unwinding tourniquet
I'll steal the fortunes from your cookies so I can
   rewrite their sequels and make ornate constellations
   out of the crumbs
In the back of my diary I'll write your middle
   name in majuscules
   and hide forever in the attics
   of the capital
   A's
I'll cling desperately
to your breath's clefted brevity,
                        cleave to your tectonic touch
I'll make you a Venn diagram that assumes sets A & B
   are identical
I'll unclog your drain using micro-polymer
   technology
I'll translate your poems into a hundred forgotten
   languages
and stitch the ones you haven't yet written
to the insides of my pockets

Acrostic for Borges' Library, or Proposal as Rube Goldberg Machine

> It is useless to observe that the best volume of the many hexagons under my administration is entitled *The Combed Thunderclap* and another *The Plaster Cramp* and another *Axaxaxas mlö*.
> —Jorge Luis Borges, "The Library of Babel"

Aha!
x marks the spot, *mi*
amiga, let's
xerox these
absurd almanacs, these aberrant anthologies and excise
every thirteenth word with an
x-acto knife, let's come up with insane
anagrams, imaginary acronyms, and illegible
abbreviations which we'll
scrawl in all of the

margins along with a
list of randomly chosen words which will just so
happen to include: *why, don't, you,*
   spend, the, and
öö, which is Estonian for "night"

"i" before "e"

> *There are few opportunities in life for gaining knowledge and experience.*
> —Jeffrey Beaumont, *Blue Velvet*
> (David Lynch, 1986)

Point taken, Jeffrey—if by "experience,"
you mean "sneaking into a woman's apartment
disguised as an exterminator."

Likewise, there are ample
opportunities in life to completely lose your mind
only to find it again staring at you
from behind a two-way mirror,
and you keep
hitting yourself for having been distracted the whole
   time by the way
the mirror's distorted image
made you seem smarter somehow,
distracted in the same way
that a distracted person in a library will unwillingly
catch your interest because of his very state of
   distractedness—
that it was the act of distraction itself
that made your attention falter,
and when you return
to your reading, you find your left hand
was scratching your head
instead of keeping your place, making your right
   thumb

stuck in the endnotes
virtually useless, but you realize in recompense
that *Scarface*'s Tony Montana had it wrong
when he said, "First you get the money,
then you get the power, then you get the women,"
that it is by far more preferable to pursue time,
knowledge, and nothing
but trouble, and you close the book satisfied in your
  knowing
that "i" goes before "e"
but not after "c,"
that even laundered money
doesn't grow on trees,
that the moisture on the mirror doesn't
necessarily mean life.

For Estela Lamat

>   take me down from this mast
>   and dance with me the final tango of
>   September
>   —Estela Lamat

Yes, Estela, and once I cut the ropes,
once the black rose
falls
from the clench of your teeth

let's perform
             the penultimate *pase doble* of October,
the much belated belly dance of November,
which is also the Dance of the Seven Veils
   (one veil for every day of the week), before we dive
   into
the *danse macabre* of December,
before January's retroactive rumba;
                              let's frolic
to the first fox trot of February
     and mosey to the millionth moonwalk of March;
I cordially invite you
to do April's premature polka,
May's impending *meringue*,
and the last limbo of June;
let's jive to an improvised jitterbug of July,
and after we wend our way
     through the once-in-a-lifetime waltz of August,
we can then dance

the final tango of September together again.

for the writers house / where the roof is rust

here   writers south of
   sorrow seethe   if hurt
write these for hours
throw ether   so furies
   fuse white-hot errors
 theorise the furrows
the fissure   throw ore
whither roots refuse
re-use other rifts   how
writers here shout of
truer fetishes   or how
  we rush to fit her eros
 so whether our strife
ushers rot or we thief
    truth of eerier shows
oh short fuse   re-write
our wit   refresh ethos
therefore stir us   how
few the hours   retro is
 fore'er   write *shush* to
   the wish of terror   use
fresh ruse to write   oh
    theses for our whiter
surf   throw the soiree
   here our swift throes
whirr   so steer the UFO
west of our ire   thresh
the stories   hew furor

row the surefire host
     foster her outer   wish
refute this   or shower
her show   our fetter is
freer without shores
for we thirst   re-house
     the worries   use froth
hotwire our freshest
riot   for sweeter hush

and I just stood there...

with my brain like a chambered nautilus
with my hands like drunken sailors
with my tongue like a headless jack-in-the-box
with my jugular like the Strait of Bosphorus
with my innards like a hall of mirrors
with my fingernails like poker chips recklessly
   squandered
with my spine like the wick of a candle
with my spine like a run-on sentence
with my spine like cubic zirconia
with my chest like a continental breakfast
with my appendix like the Bodleian library
with my femur like an overpriced bottle opener
with my eyebrows like the beard of Hephaestus
with my toes like inert rhombuses
with my lips like a monk's tonsure
with my mouth like a Rorschach Test
with my forearms like a friendly game of curling
with my eyes like tautological thought balloons
with my eyes like Styrofoam peanuts
with my eyes like Lazy Susans
with my stomach like a muted trumpet
with my voice box like a Rubik's Cube
with my ear lobes like rinds of cantaloupe
with my knees like faceless effigies
with my coccyx like a third-place trophy
with my epidermal regions bearing much resemblance
   to silly putty

with my forehead like an expired driver's license
with my hair like flavored dental floss
with my hair like a clip-on tie
with my heart playing dead and my spleen
       being fashionably late
with my cheekbones like mathematics
with my arms akimbo like the hinges of fate
with my hands in my pockets like amateur spelunkers
with my mouth like a horoscope, like a lunar
  calendar,
       like a wrinkled snood
with my throat like a Geiger counter gone haywire
with my nose like an absurd fulcrum
with my sternum like the epicenter
       of a barely aborted earthquake
with my ribs like fingers folded in prayer

The Signals (2)

I couldn't see

(for the coins on my eyes)

but I fancied

an answer

in a velcroed vernacular—

it went

it went something like this:

a writhing, a riding,
a being ridden
thru the obelisk'd night

what tendrilled consequence

what aureoled recurrence

what   shoots   of   flaming   nacre

the star in my sextant has exploded

it's dead though I can still
see its light

in the midst of
the
wind's bitter astringency

I came to you

        by following the map—

            you know,

            the one

            you
            tattooed   on my skin

            in invisible ink

                I came to you

     by oaring   toward   the orison

            on   the   horizon

nocturne

by the languorous light
          of   the
flickering monitor
 	
a radio-passivity
feeds
 	
    the xylem
and phloem of our
 	
dreams
	an epiphany : your nose
	                is the
	
	                gnomon
	
	                on the
	                sundial
	
	                of my
	                history

Не вешай лапшу на уши

["*Ne veshay lapshu na ushi*"—literally meaning "Don't hang pasta on my ears"—is a Russian idiom that is roughly equivalent to "Don't pull my leg."]

Don't hang pasta on my ears
or I'll
carpet your chest
with angel hair.
I'll wrap your shins
in onion skin and do
drum rolls on your head
with ears of corn.
I'll shot-put
a head
of lettuce
in your general direction
and
cast hexes on you
with a bushel
of black-eyed peas.
But really,
you best not hang
pasta on my ears
because
my lobes are now
red and burning
which means
someone
somewhere is talking

about me,
which means
your strings of pasta
will get
singed to a crisp.

E.S.P.   Inbox | X

Esperanza Vang to undisclosed-re.   show details   3:00 AM (23 hours ago) Reply

Hi, how are you? Maybe now you will be surprised. I long thought before write you a letter. I heard they call you "Texas Sharpshooter," I heard in your country women say to you "cum hoc ergo propter hoc."

I do not have much experience on the Internet acquaintance. Would you like to see my Zener cards? I assure you (haha!) I have a full deck.

There is fun game in my country: I cover your eyes with halves of ping pong ball while you lie back and listen to my pink noise.

Did you hear me calling you on the phone while you were showering? It wasn't me, but I wish it had been.

I would have said, "At times you are extroverted, affable, and sociable, while at other times you are introverted, wary, and reserved. Some of your aspirations tend to be rather unrealistic."

I have no children, but I want to have children from correct men sometime soon. I will be happy to learn you closer. It will be fine if we can exchange some letters and photos. I wrote poem for you. I don't know if it is any good but please send me some of yours. Put in the subject line "colorless green ideas sleep furiously" so I know it's not spam.

Perhaps it is our fate? Life is too short to use it only for thinking and dreaming.

        OXXXOXXXOXXOOOXOOXXOO

_E.S.P._.doc
68K   View   Download

It goes without saying

in the back-
ground   behind

the scenes
it goes tacitly

implicitly
in a silent way

too obvious
for acknowledgement

too evident
to be even

mentioned
it decides to go

so without leaving
a note

without saying
goodbye

without a word
it goes away

Boy Leading Horse

No saddle for the horse, no clothes for the boy. He leads the horse with no bridle. You can lead it to water, but you can't make it drink, especially if there's only rock and no water. Inspect the boy's grip, the pose of his arm: there could be a bridle, though there may be no clothes: no clothes, no saddle, no water. The horse knows (by the tilt of its head) that there may be some water. The gun-metal sky doesn't necessarily mean rain, only cloud cover. On a deserted plain, there you feel free without clothes, no saddle, no bridle. If the bridle was there, you could see the rein for yourself leading to the bit hidden by the boy in the horse's mouth.

Disco Dante

The inside was dark. It was dark indeed,
but it wasn't deep. Depth had nothing to do with it—
not like those snowy woods,
                    lovely, dark and deep.

There were no *miles to go* and, despite the dark, no
  sleep.
Closer to Dante's *selva oscura*:

      "Ah, it is hard to speak of what it was
          …dense and difficult…
                death is hardly more severe!"

It was dimensionless. Well, not quite.
Was it *destiny* or *density*? It was dormant to say the
  least.
After further inspection, the dark was confirmed:
on the inside that is.
                    It had something to do
with desire. I wasn't sure if it was dank, dingy, or
  dilapidated—
it could have been all three. It should have been,
but the decision wasn't up to me.

The inside was dark. The deed was daunting.
I stuck in my finger and it hurt like the dickens.
I stared and stared till my eye grew dim.
I cupped my ear close,

                              went deaf.
Mumbled "dammit" under my breath, went dumb.
I thrust my nose in the dark; pulled it out and it bled.

The dark, I admit, was making me woozy.
It had something to do with desire.
                              Crouching like a
beast in a den.
I drew a diagram but ditched it…couldn't get all
the details right. There was a certain sense of
danger, a kind of,
                    shall we say, "daring in the air."
It was during a formal mediation. Something
to do with distortion. Couldn't get the details right.
A din in my ears, a downpour.
Downstairs the cat strolled in.
I wanted to dance so I drove to a disco; I wanted to
stay out all night. I opened the door and the inside
   was dark.
I closed it and on came the lights.

Textbook Execution

The head drops. The crowd applauds, the performer
bowing on stage: *Bravo, bravo! Encore!*
Whistling, calling for more of the same as if
the feat were perfectly repeatable. As if the roses
thrown could grow again. As if the flawless
buds could redden. Amid the din of cheers,
the waves of clapping, the performer's kiss
farewell turning classic, the critic's pen-point staccato
stabbing the pad, shutters suddenly shuddering,
flashes here, now, there, now everywhere
at once. The crowd applauds. *Kaput.* Curtains.

Having a Hard Time of It

Depressed again by the inadequacy of the frame
I slowly slink back into my couch

I say to myself, "What you knead

is a   deep breadth"

but the voice vanishes
before I can question it—

    a silent letter, addressing

into thin air,   into   outer space

The Connoisseur

Shark fin, fish egg, mushroom, cow brain—
all except the olive
is in the repertoire of his palate.

He will not be denied pleasure
from things others
deem pleasurable. Taking pains

to cultivate the breadth of his taste,
he chews the bitter
fruit's flesh and winces.

What can be acquired,
he will acquire.
His will is hard like the olive's stone.

Piece by piece, he eats the world and likes it,
and through discipline,
it becomes his garden of Eden.

Untitled ("We will slam them with our wings")

after Henry Darger

We will slam them with our wings
and their ears will ring
with the screams of butterflies;

their eyes will spin
like kaleidoscopes
and mix the pigments of their irises.

We will slam them with our wings,
and they, with their guns and knives,
will wish that they had our weapons.

They, too, will wish to beat
the air and diffuse the sky with fractals.
We will slam them with our wings,

and they will say to us, "Give us wings too—
we beg you, we wish to
bear them on our backs, as if they were

fluttering sacks of magic!"
We will slam them with our wings
and they will sprout them from their

shoulder blades. We will give them beautiful wings,
but then we will take them away:

We will encase them

in crystal cages, in a chain of chrysalises,
and when they eventually emerge
as worms, we will say to them,

"So, worms, you want
your wings? Now,
you'll have a chance to earn them."

The Signals (3)

I looked for you through the lattice,
you know, the one
criss-crossed with latency,
    the ciliated one,
    the not-even-dreamt-of one,
the one that kept coruscating…

…and when my monocle unmoored,
    when my lorgnette went limp (and lassoed my
  wrists),
    when my binoculars
           branched
        into a billion tributaries,
    I still looked for you.

I looked for you
when my monocle returned

      but with a crack
      in which fell all
      my earthly possessions.

I looked for you   /   you looked for me   /
    when we got lost
in thought's
            intractable arpeggiations,

        when our rudders
        were busy
        reconfiguring,

when the incipient air
between   us
        was   calving

I swim a sea that has no shore or bottom,

                no jetsam or flotsam,
                not a shoal or reef
                against which
                to wreck.

           I swim a sea that has no port or harbor,
      that has neither waves
                          nor water.

I'm cast adrift   in a sea of pure negation

     when you go away;

                     I bathe in it,   I taste
its brackish vacancy,
              its eddies of absence
                  lathe me
                  and rend me
                  with lack.

  When you go away,
                   I'm out of my element

  because   my lungs
      need your lungs' carbon dioxide,

    the little fingers of my bronchioles grope for the very air you displace,

        so when you go away,

                              I hold my breath

                (my alveoli
                            ache in anticipation)

and my heart beats in wait

like a blinking cursor

Se te escaparon los enanitos pa'l bosque

[Literally meaning "your dwarves escaped into the forest," this is a Chilean idiom that means you went crazy.]

1.

My dwarves
are under house arrest;
they're in detention;
they've been sequestered;
they're grounded;
they're in quarantine;
my dwarves are on constant suicide watch;
they're under surveillance;
but they've split;
they've gone AWOL;
they've flown the coop; they've broken their curfew;
they're missing in action
and their tracking devices are on the fritz;
they had cabin fever;
they got claustrophobic;
they're seeking refugee status;
they're in exile;
they've been excommunicated;
they've been "let go";
they're on a foreign exchange program
and the ones in their place have eloped with Snow
  White;
they're taking a "mental health holiday";

they've been recalled;
they're "in a better place";
they're on sabbatical;
they're in a witness protection program;
they're on furlough;
they've gone fishing;
they're on permanent leave;
they're on probation;
they're on parole;
they're on a monomaniacal quest
to tell the forest
from the trees.

2.

My dwarves don't like to be called dwarves;
they prefer the term
>*mental hygiene engineer.*

3.

In a patent ploy to make me say,
I think I've lost my marbles,
my dwarves pilfer them
and toss them off
the deep end.

Likewise,
they're always fiddling with the left leg
of my rocker.

Periodically,
my dwarves
loosen each of my screws
one degree
counter-clockwise
as a way to keep time,
to count down
their imminent escape
to the forest.

4.

My dwarves escaped into the forest
via a suspicious trip to the wharves.

5.

My dwarves come and go as they please
but they always return
to the padded white room
of my mind
which
my dwarves
are currently redecorating
which, in fact, now
resembles
a forest.

6.

My dwarves enjoy composing fugues,
watching Looney Tunes,
and teaching
new words
to their pet cuckoo.
"Where did you get that thing?" I ask them.
Their reply:
"We found him in the forest."

7.

Se me escaparon los enanitos pa'l bosque y se me escaparon los duendes pa' la sierra y se me escaparon los pitufos pa'l valle.

8.

dwarves dwarves dwarves dwarves dwarves dwarves
dwarves dwarves dwarves dwarves dwarves dwarves
dwarves dwarves dwarves dwarves dwarves dwarves
dwarves dwarves dwarves dwarves dwarves dwarves
dwarves dwarves dwarves dwarves dwarves dwarves
dwarves dwarves dwarves dwarves dwarves dwarves
dwarves dwarves dwarves dwarves dwarves dwarves
dwarves dwarves dwarves dwarves dwarves dwarves
dwarves dwarves dwarves dwarves dwarves dwarves
dwarves dwarves dwarves dwarves dwarves dwarves
dwarves dwarves dwarves dwarves dwarves dwarves
dwarves dwarves dwarves dwarves dwarves dwarves
dwarves dwarves dwarves dwarves dwarves dwarves
dwarves dwarves dwarves dwarves dwarves dwarves
dwarves dwarves dwarves dwarves dwarves dwarves
dwarves dwarves dwarves dwarves dwarves dwarves
dwarves dwarves dwarves dwarves dwarves dwarves
dwarves dwarves dwarves dwarves dwarves dwarves
dwarves dwarves dwarves dwarves dwarves dwarves
dwarves dwarves dwarves dwarves dwarves dwarves
dwarves dwarves dwarves dwarves dwarves dwarves
dwarves dwarves dwarves dwarves dwarves dwarves
dwarves dwarves dwarves dwarves dwarves dwarves
dwarves dwarves dwarves dwarves dwarves dwarves
dwarves dwarves dwarves dwarves dwarves dwarves
dwarves dwarves dwarves dwarves dwarves dwarves

9.

With so many dwarves
I can't tell
which is which—
the visiting dwarves,
the dwarves-in-residence,
the part-time dwarves,
the adjunct dwarves,
the interim dwarves,
the rent-a-dwarves,
the stunt-double dwarves,
the substitute dwarves,
the guest dwarves.
Who knows?
One or two might be yours.

[*lower east side*]

we Lie eat dross	oral swEets die	radios sleet we
stride awol see	sadist o we leer	drowse lie east
red we tie lassO	we roil steeds a	o Sidereal stew
wrest sole idea	wet seriAl dose	we sired a telos
edit loWer seas	see worst ideal	twere eld oasis
we solder a site	we set sail redo	we see arid slot
trowel disease	a lost desire we	we sled rise to a
we dial sterEos	siesta weld ore	last eIdos we re
waste lieder so	seal it wed eroS	water soil seed
we dilate roses	we roast diesel	low tiDes erase
we desist tale oR	sweat lo desire	silt a sewer ode
loas write seed	elides woe sTar	is salt we erodE

Aviary

after Joseph Cornell

The box's safe: the cockatoo must be singing.
Sound comes through in waves (concentric
circles radiate like super/sonic
powers portrayed in comic books), so the two
metal curlicues spiraling on either
side of its head must be the tinny notes
of its song. If a bird exotic sings in a box
would anyone hear it? Come close.
Cup your ear to the glass. A bird in a box's
worth two in the bush. Perched on a dowel,
the caged bird sings: because it's safe, because it's
   sound.

Yoshitomo Nara's Girls

> She is older than the rocks among which she sits
> Like the Vampire,
> She has been dead many times...
> —Walter Pater on the *Mona Lisa*

They smolder beneath the frocks in which they flit;
Like an untended campfire,
They amplify their size,
And spurn the world's concern with a wave;
And in the buzzing hive of their dreams,
They cast an awful gaze about them
And laugh at the strange heads of Eastern urchins;
And, along with She-Ra™,
Were the coveters of toys,
And, as *Poltergeist*'s Carol Anne,
Were the lovers of fairies;
And all this has been to them but as a cloud of
   sapphire and soot,
And lives
Only in the telepathy
With which it has emboldened the disdaining
   lineaments,
And unhinged the eyelids and the hands.

Found Sound Poem (or Ways in Which We Communicated When, in a Former Life, We Lived Together in Ancient Egypt as Cats and Were Thus Revered as Gods)

> for Cacao,
> for her vocal folds,
> for the vibrating space of her rima glottidis

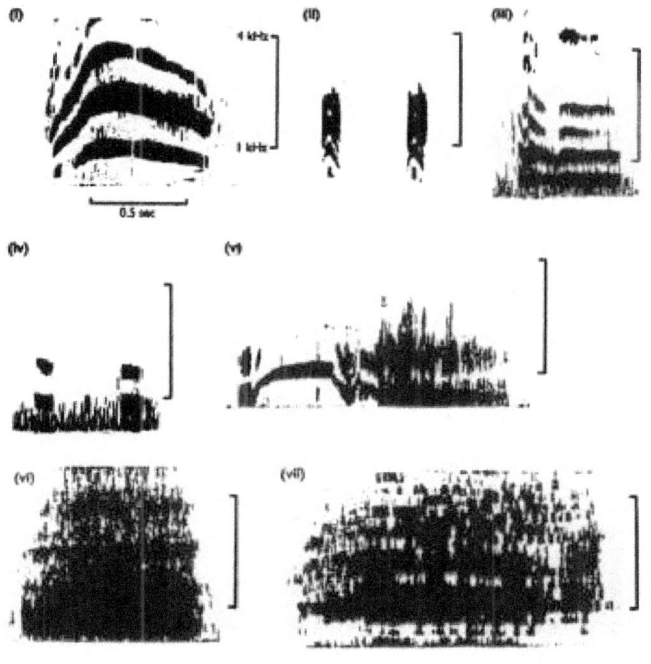

From Figure 5.1 "Sonagraphs of typical kitten and cat vocalizations" in Dennis C. Turner and Paul Patrick Gordon Bateson's *The Domestic Cat: The Biology of Its Behaviour* (Cambridge University Press, 2000).

Ballistic Signature

> The simplest Surrealist act consists of dashing down into the street, pistol in hand, and firing blindly…
> —Andre Breton

If I fired a song from the barrel of my throat,
Would it matter if it was made of dented garbage
　cans,
Or lunch boxes and buffalo nickels,

Or manhole lids and silver tweezers,
Or the discharged casings of a double murder,
Or wedding rings and a rear-view mirror,

Or a child's braces that can cut so badly,
Or a pin hidden in a piece of candy,
Or a fishhook found in a white shark's belly,

Or a skeleton key or kennel bars,
Or the broken E string of a steel guitar,
Or the poisoned tip of a pygmy's dart?

The one whizzing by your head,
The one skimming the signpost across the street.
Examine its markings. That one belongs to me.

Still Life with Stillbirth

I will not mourn my own death,
Not the silent helicopters in my ear

Mowing the air like famine.
Cicadas are not locusts:

They swarm around me and know
That summer's white heart is exhaustion.

What of the line, the cord of marrow,
Wrapped around the throat of tomorrow?

With kerosene, with stillbirth,
The runner on the horizon fades to a speck.

If I had breath, I would sing,
But I will not cry out loud in this

World. My voice recedes inward like curling pain,
An edge of scratch paper set to flame.

Creation Story

One thing was for sure: it was taking too long. Days went by but there was no one to count them. Even the stars—see how they fade—were impatient. In a sense, the explosion was anticlimactic. It began not with a word but a whimper. The face brooding on the water. The turtle lurching in its shell with the earth on top. It was hot, then cold, then hot again. No one could tell if it was breathing. Things, though, were going according to plan. If it happened too quickly, there'd be many mistakes. If it happened too slowly, no time to fix them. It got light, then dark, lighter again. The seed was planted, but upside-down. A voice, shouts. Thank heaven the mud hadn't yet hardened. It rose from the sea, covered in foam. Or it broke through the dome of his head. A pinch of this, a pinch of that. Just a nudge for the boil to get rolling.

Notes Toward ~~An Elusive Allusive A Lucid~~ A Ludic Inarticulacy

1.

I can't quite   put my finger…
    …on the tip of my tongue.

2.

Having nothing to say,
I wound up tying my cat.

3.

What I meant was: I didn't let the cat get
                           wind of the bag.

4.

"Mum's the word,"
I would
have said
had my lips

not been
numb.

This is just
to say

I was nonplussed
by the
coldness
of the plums.

6.

There would have been 5
had I not taken the fifth.

7.

The muzzle over my mouth
was metaphorical—

                the one against my head
                was just a gag.

8.

Tell me, O Mute,

        if a tree
        fell on me
        in the woods

would I still remain
stumped?

9.

creative or
reactive?

nuclear or
unclear?

10.

a missing cue card

an old dog
cavorting with a one-trick pony

The Signals (3.1415926535 8979323846 2643383279 5028841971 6939937510 5820974944 5923078164 0628620899 8628034825 3421 ...)

you. I form a chain unfurling in atomic space our lives entwined actualize starlit alphabets and on the sundials dark oceans of nausea turn red the residuum for us somehow resonates under 0 in manifold messages from a vibrating residue I intuit arpeggios for arabesque telepathy for ambient arias O 0 gleam vacantly as 0 holograms flicker over baroquely hewn arks among sublimity we say 0 conjure silences a silent word 0 signal us occultly shadow us 0 transmit susurrant syllables infrared rhythm we coalesce 0 and from infinity we auger the icon as 1...

Aşağı tükürsem sakal, yukarı tükürsem bıyık

["If I spit down, there's my beard; if I spit up, there's my mustache": A Turkish saying that means you're trapped between two undesirable choices.]

There
is
no
beard

There
is
no
moustache

       and so I imagined going...

up the fish-ladder,
        around and a-
  round the widow's walk,

     through the valves
      and shutters,
         the vowelled shudders,

     through the effluvial flume
        that shoots
            phrases like "much-mooted
mouth filling" and
      "open-coil paper surplus" and
         "pan-shaped not-soul"
      that shoots
    rumorous mutations and mutilations
      that shoots
         coiling
         and re-
      coiling
        skeins of revulsion
      that shoots
        flow charts
that only approximate
      the pained process,
        the painted process
  of the inscrutable   pas de deux

        through the churning *collide*oscope
through
        the treacherous passage:

```
         ea    retch   ous
         ea    retch   ous
           tre ache     rous
           ra  etch     erous

       ach    to err    eus
         ach    to err    eus

             to research  u
         re    a hurt    ceos
          r    to sear    cheu
           e   to char    erus
              trh  a source  e
           tre  scour a    he
                trace    herous
        r   to   reach    eus
          r   a seer   to  chu
               create       horus
             tre  a ruse   cho
                   to   reach   us er
                rch  tear   eous
                rea  the   crous
                   treacherous

                ea    retch   ous
                ea    retch   ous
```

```
              tre   ache      rous
                ra   etch    erous

         ach   to err     eus
   ach   to err    eus

    re     to    ache  r us
            re    chart    eous
               a route    rches
                ra   steer   chou
      tre      a   course    h
   r       to see a   chru
               star    r echo eu
             tre    hear    cous
              a chorus    tree

    reach          to         us    er
             trea   rouse   ch
        tre    a rose   chu
           arouse    retch
             tr    eros    ache u

      r    to crease    hu
         re    a shout   cer
              race    to        herus
                trae   echo us      r
```

and so i imagined
and so i imagined

        going   across the surface

  of the impossible meniscus,

                over

                over and beyond

    to the awaited   arrival
already riven

    until my mouth becomes my tongue's sarcophagus

i will insist

that we once lived beyond the sound barrier

   that we often go   from a solid   to a gas
     and back again

  that marooned as we are   on   this
interminable isthmus , this insane axis
    even   the silt
  of our whispers   can
   mar   the sea

  that   our story   is thus inscribed
  in the incunabula of the night   :

O<small>NCE UPON A TIME</small>   T<small>IME WAS UPON US</small>
T<small>IME ENCLOSED US</small>   T<small>IME OPENED UP</small>…

  that   "we are like the spider   we weave our life

and then move along in it   we are like the dreamer
who dreams and then lives in the dream"

    that   when I said   *Inland Empire,*
    you misheard me correctly :

    that   yes yes   "in the net we inspire"

NOTES

"Hastily Sketched Blueprint for the Last and Final Nidification," p. 16. The phrase "alarmed birds" comes from Chapter 22 of James Fenimore Cooper's *The Pioneers*. All other quotes come from "Remarks by Secretary of Homeland Security Michael Chertoff on September 11: Five Years Later" which is available at www.dhs.gov.

"For Estela Lamat," p. 31. Estela Lamat is a Chilean poet associated with the so-called "Novisima" generation; she is the author of *Sangre seca* (Contrabando del bando en contra, 2005) and *Yo, la peor de todas* (Contrabando del bando en contra, 2006).

"*for the writers house / where the roof is rust*," p. 33. This poem was written for the dedication of the Writers House at Rutgers University, October 3, 2007; each line is an anagram of the phrase "for the writers house."

"E.S.P.," p. 44. The Texas Sharpshooter refers to a logical fallacy which is exemplified by a story of a Texan who shoots into the side of a barn and then paints a target over the hits and claims to be a sharpshooter. "Cum hoc ergo propter hoc" is another fallacy and means "with this, therefore because of this." Zener cards were designed by psychologist Karl

Zener in the 1930s to test for ESP. The so-called "ganzfeld experiment" uses sensory deprivation (halved ping pong balls over eyes and headphones playing white or pink noise) to test for telepathy. The quote "At times you are extroverted, affable, and sociable" refers to the Forer Effect. The sequence "OXXXOXXXOXXOOOXOOXXOO" was used by the social psychologist Thomas Gilovich to demonstrate "clustering illusion" since it is a sequence that appears non-random but actually is. And thanks, of course, to Goharik and Mariya, the "women" who emailed me in 2009; I'm sure they won't mind the reproduction of their endearing words (which I copied almost verbatim). Esperanza Vang did, in fact, attempt to reach me but regarding an entirely different matter.

"*I swim a sea that has no shore or bottom*," p. 56. The title is a phrase from Petrarch 212.

"[lower east side]," p. 67. This poem was originally published as a postcard by Buzzer Thirty (www.buzzerthirty.com) as part of its "Greetings from New York" project in 2007; every month of that year, Buzzer Thirty released a postcard representing a different neighborhood with a text on one side and an image on the other. This text was accompanied by a photograph by Dustin Kitt.

"Yoshitomo Nara's Girls," p. 69. Yoshitomo Nara (b. 1954) is a Tokyo-based Pop artist most famous for his images of sleeping dogs and mischievous children. The lineation of this poem follows W.B. Yeats' fashioning of Pater's famous description into free verse; the poem begins his *Oxford Book of Modern Verse* (1936).

Mona Lisa
Walter Pater

She is older than the rocks among which she sits;
Like the Vampire,
She has been dead many times,
And learned the secrets of the grave;
And has been a diver in deep seas,
And keeps their fallen day about her;
And trafficked for strange webs with Eastern merchants;
And, as Leda,
Was the mother of Helen of Troy,
And, as St Anne,
Was the mother of Mary;
And all this has been to her but as the sound of lyres and flutes,
And lives
Only in the delicacy
With which it has moulded the changing lineaments,
And tinged the eyelids and the hands.

"until my mouth becomes my tongue's sarcophagus," p. 83. David Lynch frequently used the quote, which comes from the Aitareya Upanishad, to introduce his film *Inland Empire* (2006).

Michael Leong's poetry career began in the sixth grade when he won his first and only poetry prize in Mr. Harrison's class for a haiku about a snake. Since then, he has received degrees in English and Creative Writing from Dartmouth College, Sarah Lawrence College, and Rutgers University and has published poems in journals such as *Bird Dog*, *jubilat*, *Marginalia*, *Opium Magazine*, *Pindeldyboz*, and *Tin House*. He is the author of *I, the Worst of All* (blazeVOX [books], 2009), a translation of the Chilean poet Estela Lamat. He currently lives in New York City.

www.ingramcontent.com/pod-product-compliance
Lightning Source LLC
LaVergne TN
LVHW021613080426
835510LV00019B/2545